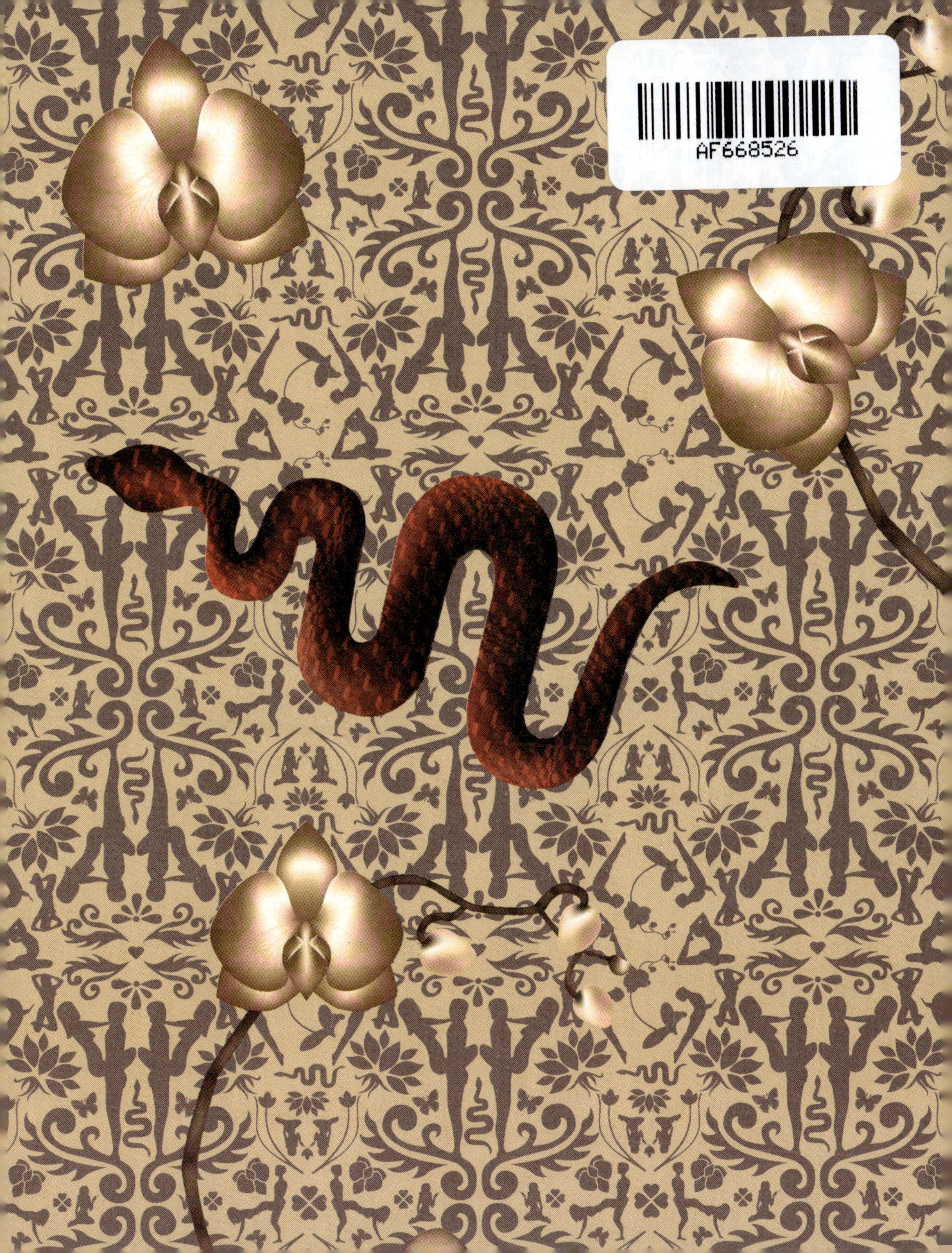

leela

First published in India in 2009 by Collins,
an imprint of HarperCollins *Publishers* India
a joint venture with
The India Today Group

135798642
ISBN: 978-81-7223-7721

HarperCollins *Publishers*
A - 53, Sector 57, Noida 201301, India
77-85 Fulham Palace Road, London W6 8JB, United Kingdom
Hazelton Lanes, 55 Avenue Road, Suite 2900, Toronto
Ontario M5R 3L2 and 1995 Markham Road, Scarborough, Ontario M1B 5M8, Canada
25 Ryde Road, Pymble, Sydney, NSW 2073, Australia
31 View Road, Glenfield, Auckland 10, New Zealand
10 East 53rd Street, New York NY 10022, USA

Printed and bound at
Thomson Press (India) Ltd.

DESIGN BY NIKKI DUGGAL DESIGN

leela

AN EROTIC PLAY OF VERSE AND ART

ALKA PANDE

Collins

To:

With love:

Contents

The Erotic Ancient 14

The Sensual Medieval 30

The Free-Spirited Contemporary 56

Acknowledgements

This has been a long journey beset with innumerable challenges. An anthology, I realize now, is even more of a challenge than writing one's own text. The nascent idea for this book can be attributed to Christine Cipriani whom I met on a cold winter evening in 2002. Over the next few years I lost myself reading innumerable texts to develop the idea. Christine went back to America and left me in the very capable hands of V.K. Karthika, who also gave me my sensitive editor, Sheema Mookherjee who brought to this book a deft nurturing hand.

Kudos are due to my young designer Nikki Duggal who immediately took on the project when I approached her. She brought in the provocative look and feel I had envisioned for the book. To all you lovely ladies my heartfelt gratitude.

Together, we decided to bring in the quintessential spirit of contemporary India where tradition and modernity walk hand in hand. Thus, I zeroed down on some modern photographers and artists who joined me in this adventure. Each one of them – Ashish Chawla, Bandeep Singh, Vikram Bawa, Akash Das, Waswo X. Waswo, Lesleigh Goldberg, Sanjib Sen and Kishore Chatterjee – took time out to send appropriate images so that I could pair them with the poetry.

Thanks to Kamla Kapur, Pritish Nandy, David Ray, Sudeep Sen, Jeet Thayil, and others who so generously gave permission to include their work in this anthology. And to Dulpreet, who spent innumerable hours searching for names, sections and publication details to facilitate copyright permissions, and also helped in securing some lyrical verses.

To my daughter Mandakini who distils the beauty in my life. Above all, to my husband who energizes every work of mine.

Alka Pande

Introduction

'Sex is need but Eros is desire'

– ROLLO MAY, EXISTENTIAL PSYCHOLOGIST

This collection of verse and images, more than anything else, is the recognition of desire. It is an exploration of how the Indian creative expression gave birth to, developed and celebrated desire through the ages. It is the expression of the erotic, which has existed since time immemorial, hidden subtly in every aspect of life.

The word 'erotica' applies to artistic and literary works in which the sexual element is woven into the larger aesthetic aspect. The word itself is a nineteenth-century invention of booksellers who wished to lend respectability to items that could be confiscated by the authorities; it was only in the twentieth century that artists began to self-consciously produce erotica.

The debate of art versus pornography (which has only one purpose: sexual arousal) is an undying one, and the fine lines drawn between the two are of a purely subjective nature. Unlike the Judaeo-Christian tradition, where the erotic is all too frequently associated with sin and guilt, the Indian tradition has been less oppressed by a rigid moral code. The popularity of the *Kamasutra*, the classic Indian text on the subject of sexuality, is evidence of a relatively liberal tradition. As Sir Richard Francis Burton, who made the first English translation of the *Kamasutra* available to European readers in 1883, observed in his introduction: 'In Hinduism, sex is almost sacramental, essential to human life, and therefore worthy of serious study.'

This anthology combines verse and visual art to provide a glimpse into the working of the erotic mind across centuries. The verse is divided into three sections, premised on the period of creation

– ancient, medieval and contemporary – and the photographs and paintings have been chosen to illustrate and complement the erotic sensibility inherent in the poetry.

In ancient India, the metaphor of sexuality was used not only in the context of lovemaking, but also as an expression of art, music and literature. In the two great epics, Ramayana and Mahabharata, desire is depicted as a matter of physical gratification. The real flowering of the concept of eroticism is reflected in the literature of the Sangam period, the works of Kalidasa, and the *Kamashastra* – the generic name for the classic love texts, including the *Kamasutra*.

The medieval period shows the influence of the Bhakti movement as well as of Sufism, which left an indelible mark on poetry – much of it romantic in colour and used to express sacred love. Later, in the Mughal era, the pleasure principle was refined to a fine art, as reflected in the miniature paintings and the poetry of the period, with its nuanced tilt towards the erotic.

The contemporary age has seen a qualitative change in erotic expression: it appears to be driven by the urge for personal fulfilment. One sees an emphasis on the exploration of sexuality and identity, the acknowledgement of female equality and desire, as well as the freedom to choose the object of desire, regardless of the proprieties of sex/gender.

The Erotic Ancient

Myths, allegories and metaphors

Beginning with yoni worship and phallic traditions, India abounds in the symbology of the sacred erotica. At the heart of most mythologies are sensuous stories of the gods making love, which also reflect the power and purpose of human passion. In Hinduism, Shakti, the consort of Shiva, is the emblem of feminine cosmic creativity, the counterpart to his lingam or phallus: Shaiva temples have a circular yoni pedestal for the lingam.

Drawing on amorous myths, as well as the oldest treatises on love, we can deduce that the erotic element was a common recurring pattern in the Indian cultural tradition too. As were the twin themes of sexuality and spirituality, which are inextricably woven into the mythology and literary texts of ancient India.

The other ancient philosophy, of Tantra – which literally means 'to expand the mind' – teaches one to experience the absolute through the path of the flesh. The various Tantric schools assert that just as the world is real, so is the body, and the Tantric practice of sadhana continually directs attention back to the physical self.

Whether it is the individual or the divine Other that forms the subject of literary and artistic creation during this period, it appears that the aspect of sexuality was dealt with explicitly and scientifically. Hence, the production of the erotic manual *Kamasutra*, and great poetic works such as *Kokashastra, Anangaranga, Nimmat Nama*; the Aham poetry of the Tamil kingdoms; the works of Kalidasa; as well as the bold mention of sexuality in music, dance and art.

And constantly, underlying it all, there is the reminder that human existence is nothing more than leela, or the divine play of the gods.

The *Kamashastra*

The sage Babhravpanchal is said to have compiled the *Kamashastra*, which later scholars divided into different volumes. The *Kamasutra* is believed to be an abridged version of this work. Written more as a manual for householders, the *Kamasutra* is truly a set of aphorisms on love. And it would not be wrong to say that the roots of all Indian erotic literature lie embedded in this fourth-century text, which is commonly attributed to the sage Vatsyayana.

The *Kamasutra* is a book on sexology that also contains a colourful record of the social and cultural life of the period. Along with the other love texts such as *Kokashastra, Anangaranga* and *Saundaryalahiri*, it was to become a perennial influence on the creative arts in subsequent centuries.

Written at the same time as the *Kamashastra*, during the Gupta rule in northern India, *Natya Shastra*, the bible of dramaturgy, introduced the rasa theory to the world. It shed light on the eight rasas or aesthetic experiences. Among them is shringara rasa – also known as the rasaraja or the king of all rasas – encompassing within it every aspect of love and desire. It is shringara that legitimizes the appreciation of the nude, and other expressions of love and desire within the Indian cultural consciousness.

The other major influence on future erotic work was the poetry of the Sangam period, broadly classified into Aham meaning 'interior' or love poems; and Puram meaning 'exterior' or poems on war. Another poetic work of the second century, *Gathasaptasati*, is remarkable for its descriptions of female sensuality. Interestingly, these are accounts of active sexual participation and not the passive conduct one might expect from a more conservative social order.

The magic of Kalidasa

The finished epic form in classical literature, however, did not evolve until the time of Kalidasa, around the fifth century. Considered the king of all poets, Kalidasa evocatively describes love and courtship in his works – *Meghaduta* and *Kumarasambhava* in particular. His poem *Ritusamhara* or 'The Cycle of Seasons' is the distilled essence of the pure love of a newly married couple, expressed in terms of overflowing joy. This poem is divided into six books, corresponding to the six seasons. Apart from a vivid account of the changing seasons, the sentiments that they evoke in lovers are described with great passion. Kalidasa's works mark the zenith of erotic literature in the classical period.

Your hairs rise up when you're kissed
and your goose bumps break out.
Quit feigning sleep
(I : 23) and I'll do it the way you like it.

Why do you scorch my back
with your sighs
while I wait for a touch of your breast?
(I : 33) The night mocks our effort at anger.

With her eyes closed
she brought him to bed in her mind,
then did all the work with her hands
(II: 33) till her jingling bangles fell slack.

When the lady's on top
her hair's a splendid curtain, swaying.
Her ear-rings dangle, her necklace shakes.
(V: 46) And she's busy, bee on a lotus-stalk.

When they stopped
she was embarrassed by her nakedness
but since she couldn't reach her clothes
(V: 59) she pulled him upon her once more.

From Gathasaptasati

Bandeep Singh

Summer

Sweating all over at each subtle joint, young damsels put away their heavy clothes, and wear light skills about their buxom breasts. (I. 7)

The Rains

Sweet maidens ravish their lovers, with their long hair, decked with fragrant flowers, reaching to their hips, with glitter of pearls on their breasts, their faces flushed with wine. (II. 18)

Early Winter

The cold season is shedding tears of dewdrops on blades of grass, distressed at the weight of lovers on luscious bosoms, his favourite snug resort. (IV. 7)

Spring

The cuckoo is drunk with mango nectar and kisses his mate with passionate fervour. The buzzing drone on the lotus flower sings a love song in praise of his beloved bee. (VI. 14)

From Ritusamhara: Kalidasa

Waswo X. Waswo

'...As you, black and glossy as a maiden's plait, rest on the mountain peak, its sides all yellow with ripe wild mangoes, the divine couples moving in the sky will enjoy the sight as if they saw Earth's broad breast, white all round and tipped with black.'

Ashish Chawla

From Meghaduta: Kalidasa

Lesleigh Goldberg

On a single couch he saw his ladies
    not just one, but two;
The rogue crept up behind them
    he knew just what to do;
One lady's eyes he covered up
    as if to play 'Guess Who?'
He turned to kiss the other one
    she blushed, a merry hue;
But she held back her laughter
    and the other never knew.

In the morning:
    the armlet's imprint was on his neck,
    the black mascara was on his face,
    the red betel stain was on his eyelids,
    the mark of lac was on his forehead –
For a long while she looked at her beloved's
    adornments, incitements to anger, and then
The young girl sighed into a lotus,
    The flower with which she had been playing.

'But your eyes are wet: why are they red?'
'The words of your lover filled me with dread.'
'But your hair is dishevelled, why such a mess?'
'The wind was blowing, I have to confess.'
'And your makeup, all gone, rubbed all away?'
'Yes, rubbed off by the shawl I was wearing today.'
'But your breathing is heavy; why are you tired?'
'From working so hard, doing what you desired.'
'Very clever, my friend, you've not made a slip,
So tell me what rhymes with the bite on your lip.'

Confrontations: Amarusataka

Vikram Bawa

Tight-embraces-crushed-breasts-bristling-delight-
Intense-love-swelling-felling-girdle-skin-slipping-
Faint-whispers:
no
no
too much
no
don't
no
enough
no . . .
'Is he asleep? Is she dead? Or has she disappeared
melted absorbed
into my heart...?'

Unions: Amarusataka

Lesleigh Goldberg

The Sensual Medieval

By the tenth century, the depiction of sex in art had entered a qualitatively new phase. Erotic motifs were no longer confined to hidden spaces in temples. All forms of sexual activity between men and women, gods and goddesses, aristocrats and ascetics, were displayed ostentatiously on the exteriors of temples. India's unique gift of adventurous love to the world – the Khajuraho temples – were erected between AD 950 and 1050. Khajuraho was also the centre of one of the most esoteric religious traditions of India – Tantra. The sculptures and paintings seen at Bhubaneshwar, Konark, Sanchi, Nagarjunakonda and Ajanta are further expressions of this renaissance in erotic art and literature.

In the eleventh century, the Kashmiri poet Bilhana composed a significant body of sensual and secular work, in the form of miniature or fragmentary lyrics (Khandakavya). According to legend, he had a secret affair with the king's young daughter whom he was supposed to be instructing on the subtleties of literature. When they were discovered, the king condemned him to death. In the moments before his execution, he evoked the princess in lyric verse whose beauty was so powerful that the goddess Kali interceded with the king to grant him pardon. Bilhana's compositions are spun together in a collection of fifty verses known as *Chaurapanchasika*.

Adoring the beloved

The poet-philosophers of the Bhakti movement, such as Vidyapati, Surdas, Tulsidas and Meera saw no contradiction in donning the garb of a lover, friend, child or parent while addressing their chosen deity. In many ways, this represents a pluralistic understanding of intimacy, foreshadowing modern psychologists' perceptions that the beloved is never just one thing.

It is also representative of the Indian philosophical tradition that suggests a structural unity of the cosmos through the union between man and god, the individual essence and the universal force, the lover and the beloved.

The poetry that arose from the deeply spiritual Bhakti movement rejected the elite tradition of Sanskrit and gave an impetus to the development of regional languages. It also challenged the existing caste system as many of its poets were from the

lower castes, and a common theme in their poetry was that god resides within every human being.
In the twelfth century was written another great erotic text: Jayadeva's *Gita Govinda*. The stories of love between Radha and Krishna had existed in folklore for years, but Jayadeva created a web of romance and sensuality that lifted the relationship into sublime universality. Resonating with melody and visual imagery, *Gita Govinda* explains the universe through the basic principle of love.

In the later Bhakti era came the genre of Ritikavya, which expressed a harmonious relationship between spirituality and sensuality. Unlike Bhaktikavya, which was devotional in nature, Ritikavya added a worldly dimension to the Radha-Krishna poetry.

Then came the sixteenth-century poet Keshavdas's monumental work *Rasikpriya*, a celebrated treatise on the erotic. The book deals with different kinds of nayaks and nayikas (heroes and heroines), their lovemaking, moods, sentiments and emotions. The popularity of this work among the royalty and nobility was furthered by its depiction in miniature paintings and various other artistic renditions.

The age of pleasure

In the middle of the sixteenth century, Akbar's generous patronage of art and poetry gave rise to the Mughal school of art, and love for the sake of pure pleasure began to be celebrated. Akbar's successors, Jahangir and Shah Jahan, continued to actively patronize the arts with particular emphasis on the sensuous and romantic.

The later Mughal era gave rise to new schools of Rajasthani miniature painting. Although influenced by the Mughal style, they were Rajput in spirit and drew inspiration from Sanskrit and Hindi classics such as *Gita Govinda, Rasamanjari* and *Rasikpriya*.

While the erotic element in art was expressed in miniature paintings, romantic poetry found expression in the Sufi compositions of the period. The verses of Amir Khusro are charged with romance and the erotic imagination, and represent a high point in the tradition of Perso-Urdu poetry.

Even now,
I regret her –
gleaming in garlands of gold champac
flowers,
her lotus face blossoming,
the line of down delicate at her waist,
her body trembling and eager for love
when she wakes from sleep –
magic I lost somehow in recklessness.

Even now,
if I see her again,
a lotus-eyed girl
weary from bearing her own heavy
breasts –
I'll crush her in my arms
and drink her mouth like a madman,
a bee insatiably drinking a lotus!

Even now,
if I see her again,
wide-eyed,
fevered from long parting –
I'll lock her tight in my limbs,
Close my eyes, and never leave her!

Even now,
I remember her,
holding the reins
in our wild dance of love,
moon lustre lighting her face,
her body trembling with passion –
delicate
Bent by lush breasts and heavy hips,
Dancing mantled in a mane of flying hair.

Even now,
I remember her lying in bed,
Spreading perfume of musk
Mixed with sandalwood oils –
Her seductive eyelashes playing
Like a pair of mating birds
Caressing each other's bills.

Even now,
I remember the wine-smeared lips
she innocently licked in love,
her frail form, her wanton long eyes,
her body rubbed golden
with saffron paste and musk,
her mouth spiced
with camphor and betel nut.

Even now,
I remember my love's face:
golden earrings
gnawing her cheeks
as she strove
to take the man's role,
beads of sweat strewn thick
like pearls
from the toil
of her rhythmic swinging.

Even now,
I remember her bold bent glance,
her graceful limbs stretching
in pleasure,
her voluptuous breasts' curve
bared by slipping clothes,
her lip bruised with marks of my teeth.

Even now,
I remember the mark of my nail left
on her sandalwood-powdered thigh –
the gold-streaked cloth I snatched
when she rose
was clutched in shame as she
  pulled away.

Even now,
I remember in secret
her braid's loosened ties,
wilted garlands,
nectar-sweet smiling lips,
strands of pearls
caressing luscious swollen breasts,
and longing looks.

Even now,
I remember her eyes
trembling, closed after love,
her slender body limp,
fine clothes and heavy hair loose –
a wild goose
in a thicket of lotuses of passion.
I'll remember her in my next life
and even at the end of time!

Even now,
I remember the love-play battle
she fought with empty hands
in rising falling rhythms,
wet with hot red blood
from tooth marks on her lips
and nail marks on her body –
her tyranny bewitched me in the bout.

Fantasies of a Love Thief: Bilhana

Kishore Chatterjee

In spring when the love lord's golden staff is seen in the colour of *kesara* flowers,
When bees which come to the clustering *patala* make that flower the quiver of love,
Hari here in the forest dwells, in eager dance with the women folk –
It is hard to endure being parted in spring, my friend!

In spring when youthful *karuna* trees look laughing at those who lose their shame,
When spear-shaped boughs are studding the quarters, piercing those who are parted from love,
Hari here in the forest dwells, in eager dance with the women folk –
It is hard to endure being parted in spring, my friend!

In spring when blossoming mangoes thrill to the clasp of the tremulous vernal creepers,
When the Vrindavana forest is cleansed by the water of Jamna meandering through the wood,
Hari here in the forest dwells, in eager dance with the women folk –
It is hard to endure being parted in spring, my friend!

This, the description – the forest in spring-time, delightful – threaded with phases of passion,
The purpose of which is to recollect Hari, wells up in the utterance of Sri Jayadeva.
Hari here in the forest dwells, in eager dance with the women folk –
It is hard to endure being parted in spring, my friend!

From Gita Govinda: Jayadeva

You are my life, and you are my ornament,
you are the jewel, the gem,
in the depth of the ocean of all my being,
So be gracious to me, and thus continue to be, and my heart shall always
endeavour to be most worthy of you!
O loved one, O beautiful,
give up that baseless pride against me!
My heart is burnt by the fire of longing;
give me that drink
so sweet of your lotus face!

From Gita Govinda: Jayadeva

Sanjib Sen

Ashish Chawla

Vikram Bawa

Her hair, flying loose,
Veils the splendour of her face
As demonic shadow eats the radiant moon.
The flower-strings in her hair
Play careless games
And tangle together
Like twin rivers when they flood.

Ecstatic, today,
Is this exercise of love; astride
Radha is riding Krishna,
Beads of sweat shimmer on her face
Like pearls from the full moon,
Given to her as gifts
By the god of love.

With all her strength
She kisses her lover's lips,
Like the moon leaning down
To suck from a lotus bloom.
Her necklace dangles
Below her drooping breasts
As if milky streams
Dripped from their golden bowls.
The bells on her waistband jingle, and
Sing musical praises to the god of love.

Vidyapati

Ashish Chawla

Surativichitra Madhya: Keshavdas

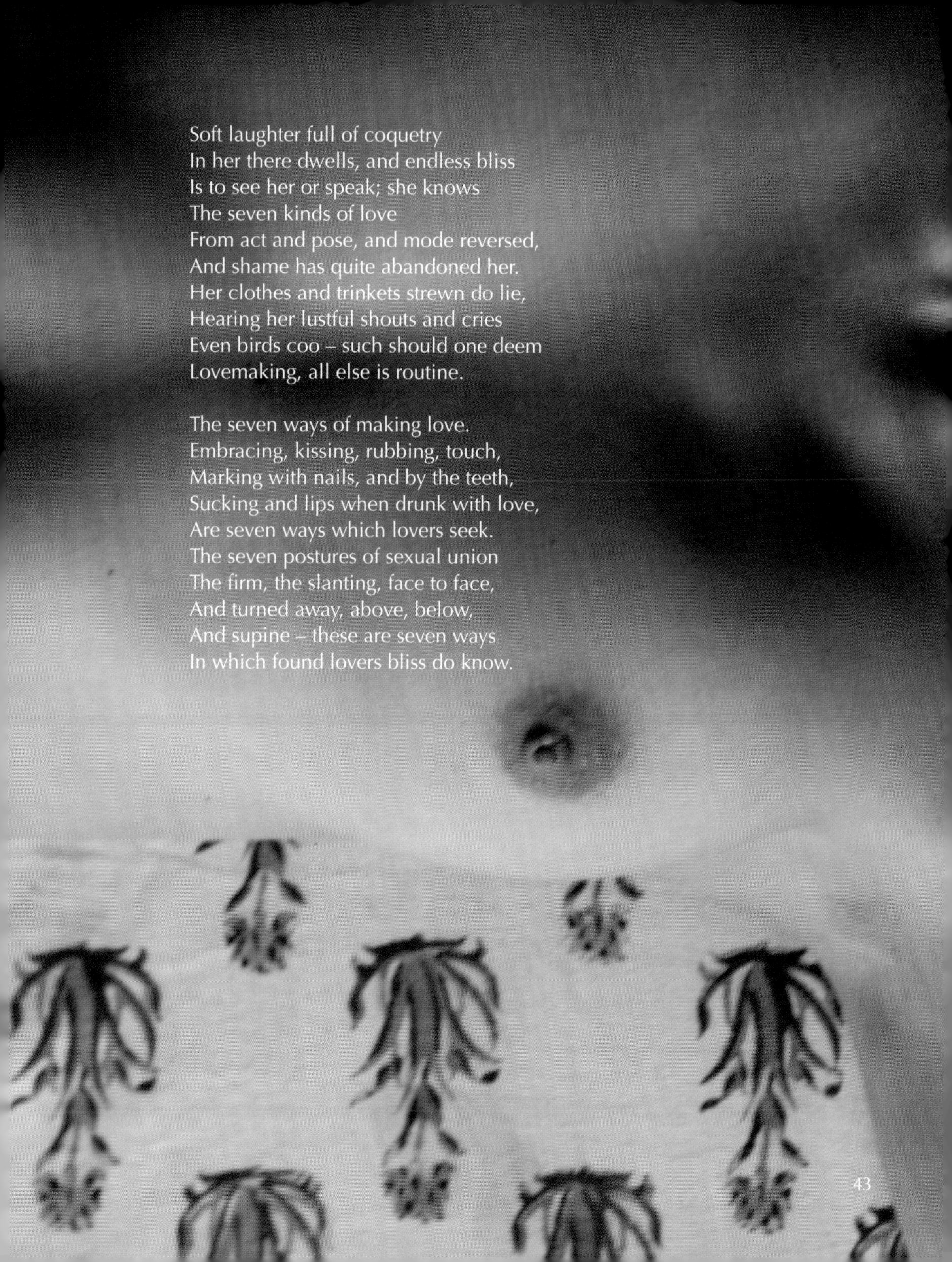

Soft laughter full of coquetry
In her there dwells, and endless bliss
Is to see her or speak; she knows
The seven kinds of love
From act and pose, and mode reversed,
And shame has quite abandoned her.
Her clothes and trinkets strewn do lie,
Hearing her lustful shouts and cries
Even birds coo – such should one deem
Lovemaking, all else is routine.

The seven ways of making love.
Embracing, kissing, rubbing, touch,
Marking with nails, and by the teeth,
Sucking and lips when drunk with love,
Are seven ways which lovers seek.
The seven postures of sexual union
The firm, the slanting, face to face,
And turned away, above, below,
And supine – these are seven ways
In which found lovers bliss do know.

That pert one drinks and then denies it to me
What am I to do for I dare not smell his breath?
I saw him once in a dream, and now for years
Every night and day I remind myself of that dream.
Only the wind can now carry my feelings to the beloved's abode
For no caravan bearing solace passes this way any more.
Alas, I am too weak to injure about him
Enough that I am lying at his door.

(129)

Amir Khusro

Kishore Chatterjee

Sanjib Sen

Waswo X. Waswo

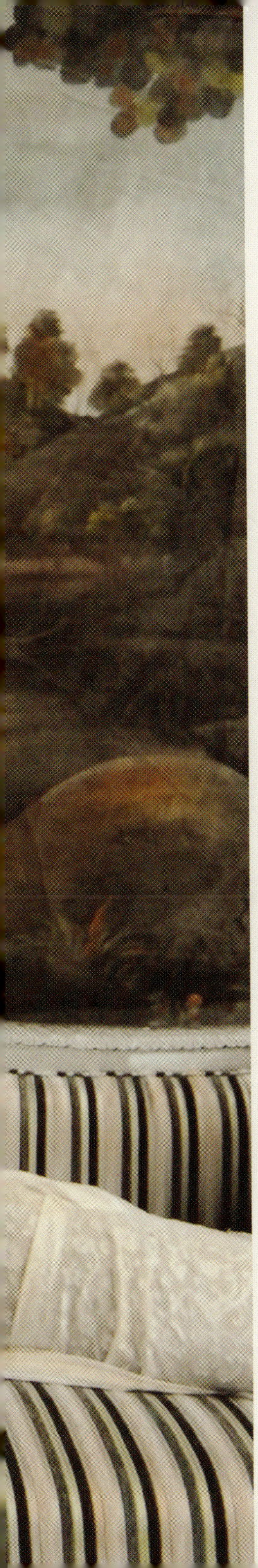

You know that Khusro is famed for his sweet words
If not for my heart's sake, come for my tongue.
(136)

The language of my beloved is Turkish, and Turkish I do not know
Would it not be wonderful if his tongue were in my mouth.

Beloved, if at night, I put my lips to yours
Pretend to be asleep – don't ask whose mouth this is.

Oh lord, is this me with my shoulder next to my beloved?
Have I been in bed sleeping by my side?
(139)

The sun that is his face scorched me from afar
It was a relief when I found the shade of his tresses.
(140)

Oh cruel one with your cap askew, whose beloved are you?
With your words of love who are you seducing now?
(142)

When Hussayn takes Madho's lips in his own
he transmits his blessing in the most intimate way.
When Madho answers his lips with shy delicacy
he coaxes from each blessing many more blessings.
Hussayn is training Madho from the depth of his soul
how to pass along the mystic path to truth…

Waswo X. Waswo

Waswo X. Waswo

Hussayn was kneeling in respect,
his eyes and his heart focussed only on Madho.
Madho took from his hand a glass of deep-hued wine –
he drank from it, and Hussayn kissed his wine-sweet lips,
Then Madho gave his glass filled to the brim
and kissed Hussayn in answer on his reddened lips.
Hussayn rose tranquilly from his place
and Madho rose as well, answering his call.
Holding his hand, Madho sat down, crossing his legs,
his face illumined with bright joy.
Hussayn handed him a goblet of sparkling wine
as if burning in a fever of ardour.
He took a sip from the goblet and gave one to Hussayn,
he accepted a kiss and gave one to Hussayn.
Hussayn rose again to give of himself more generously
and Madho graciously accepted his advances.
In this way, the lovers engaged in a play of passions,
demanding and acceding, teasing and refusing.
Each enticed the other, stirring his desire,
mingling wine and kisses like sugar dissolved in milk.
One passes the goblet like the very shape of delight
while the other accepts the gift with humble supplication.
When the other holds the cup, imploring,
he accepts the tribute, begging for even more delicacies.
In this duet of beseeching and tenderly replying
the two friends made love with each other.
Each of them in each act is captivated by the other
loving each other with the kindest intimacy.
One kisses the other with an ecstatic breath
moving from his wrist to his hand, his strong arm, his shoulder,
Then he kisses his forehead and then his cheek,
gently kisses both his eyelids and then his brows,
Then with sweet affection he kisses his lips,
with love he kisses the smooth skin beneath his chin…

Haqiqat al Fuqara

Sanjib Sen

The Free-Spirited Contemporary

In our own time, sexuality continues to be explored as enthusiastically as it was before, but with a more self-conscious sensibility. The expressions are more autobiographical and open, with the body becoming only one of the sites of erotic manifestation.

The immediate post-Independence years saw a remarkable proliferation in the number of women writers, ranging from Sarojini Naidu to Ismat Chughtai, Amrita Pritam, Kamala Das and Qurratulain Hyder. Their work made a radical shift to the realm of everyday life into which were woven undercurrents of sexuality.

And then there are the younger poets, more cosmopolitan in tone, who display an internationalism that results from frequent journeys, physical and emotional, between the West and the East, the new and the old. Often, in these younger writers, the practice of writing is itself transformed into an erotic act.

The poems in this last section, as also the images that illuminate them, have one recurring leitmotif: erotic pleasure. For, modernists everywhere, however different their forms of expression, would be in agreement that without experiencing the erotic, life is never completely lived.

I know all your fitful fancies
Leafy language, flitting footsteps,
All my boughs break into blossom
At your passing breath and whisper,
All my leaves break into tumult
Of surrender at your kisses…

Yet 'tis of you thro' the moonlit ages
That maidens and minstrels sing,
And lay your buds on the great god's altar
O radiant blossom that fling
Your rich, voluptuous, magical perfume
To ravish the winds of spring.

Champak Blossoms: Sarojini Naidu

Ashish Chawla

Akash Das

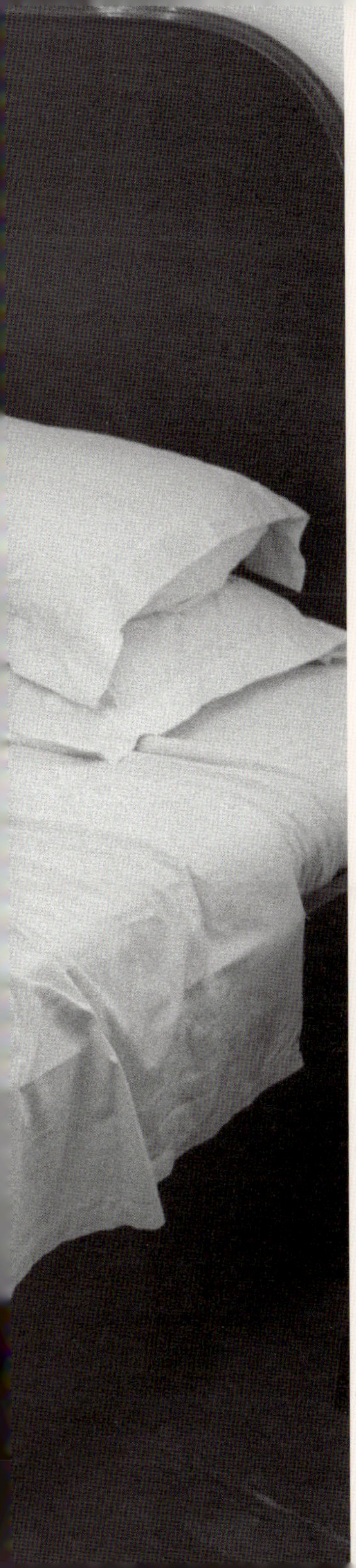

When I moved into your bed
I was not alone – there were two of us
A married woman and a virgin
to sleep with you
I had to offer the virgin in me
I did so
This slaughter is permissible in law
not the indignity of it
And I bore the onslaught of the insult
The next morning
I looked at my bloodstained hands
I washed my hands
but the moment I stood
before the mirror
I found her standing there
the one whom I thought I
had slaughtered the last night
Oh god!
Alas it being too dark in your bed
I had to kill one and I killed the other.

The Virgin: Amrita Pritam

Getting a man to love you is easy
Only be honest about your wants as
Woman. Stand nude before the glass with him
So that he sees himself the stronger one
And believes it so, and you so much more
Softer, younger, lovelier...Admit your
Admiration. Notice the perfection
Of his limbs, his eyes reddening under
Shower, the shy walk across the bathroom floor,
Dropping towels, and the jerky way he
Urinates. All the fond details that make
Him male and your only man. Gift him all
Gift him what makes you woman, the scent of
Long hair, the musk of sweat between the breasts,
The warm shock of menstrual blood, and all your
Endless female hungers. Oh yes, getting
A man to love is easy, but living
Without him afterward may have to be
Faced. A living without life when you move
Around, meeting strangers, with your eyes that
Gave up their search, with ears that hear only
His last voice calling out your name and your
Body which once under his touch had gleamed
Like burnished brass, now drab and destitute.

The Looking Glass: Kamala Das

Ashish Chawla

Fond husband, ancient settler in the mind,
Old fat spider, weaving webs of bewilderment,
Be kind. You turn me into a bird of stone, a granite
Dove, you build round me a shabby drawing room,
And stroke my pitted face absent-mindedly while
You read. With loud talk you bruise my pre-morning sleep,
You stick a finger into my dreaming eye. And
Yet, on daydreams, strong men cast their shadows, they sink
Like white suns in the swell of my Dravidian blood,
Secretly flow the drains beneath sacred cities.
When you leave, I drive my blue battered car
Along the bluer sea. I run up the forty
Noisy steps to knock at another's door.
Through peep-holes, the neighbours watch,
they watch me come
And go like rain. Ask me, everybody, ask me
What he sees in me, ask me why he is called a lion,
A libertine, ask me the flavour of his
Mouth, ask me why his hand sways like a hooded snake
Before it clasps my pubis. Ask me why like
A great tree, felled, he slumps against my breasts,
And sleeps. Ask me why life is short and love is
Shorter still, ask me what is bliss and what its price...

The Stone Age: Kamala Das

Akash Das

The slight dip of your head on the pillow, is still there
The sheets hold the moist scent of your body
My hands are fragrant with the smell of your face
On my forehead is the stamp of your lips.

You are so close that I cannot see you.
Move away a little, so I can see your face.

Distance: Gulzar

'Is this how they acted in real life?'
a tourist girl asks as she looks up
at the scene. One sandstone houri
with hemispherical breasts holds
a long penis with loving attention
and a playful smile. Another kneels.

The perspective seems to be from
above, as through a surveillance lens,
but in an ancient palace, not a motel.
The girl with her guidebook open
looks up at the scene as if she might
be in the Louvre before an old Master.

'Not at all,' says the guide in a chiding
tone, after giving her time to examine
each detail as he studies her face.
'Such behaviour is only for the gods –
and the gods, they were very naughty.'
But he licks his lips and has a playful smile.

Here in Khajuraho where I wander lonely
as a prude at an orgy the guide's tease
seems more than appropriate. I would not
even be a witness had I not been dragged off
the plane by authorities who demanded
my seat for a tour group. And there is not
another flight scheduled for days. Were
my own lover with me I would be delighted,
and the temples might simply inspire us.
But by gazing at such lovers while alone
is to be lost in awe of the transcendent
while enduring the torture of being alone.

Oh, lost lovers frozen in positions of ecstasy,
let me read 'To His Coy Mistress' to you
in moonlight, and together we may achieve
the ecstasy, the mystery, the joy lost
and then found together, embracing in stone.

At Khajuraho: David Ray

Lesleigh Goldberg

Glowing body, painted lips, magic eyes, curly hair;
Shining marble, scarlet clouds, red horizon, frightened deer.

Alms for beggars, drink for the thirsty, water for the pot, river for the sea,
Scent for the garden, song for the cuckoo, wine for the drunkard – you and me.

Cobra for the charm-pipe, shade for the yard, tinkling bells, hope for the heart,
Eyes with kohl, clouds and hills, your flowing locks, my arms apart.

Perfumed nights, burning breath, drunken eyes, rainy weather,
Dreams of beauty, toys of love, scattering flowers, we together.

Parted from you, what can I do? Wounds so deep, sleep flies away.
Lonely evenings, weaving dreams, talking to myself –
that's my way!

Ghazal: Javed Akhtar

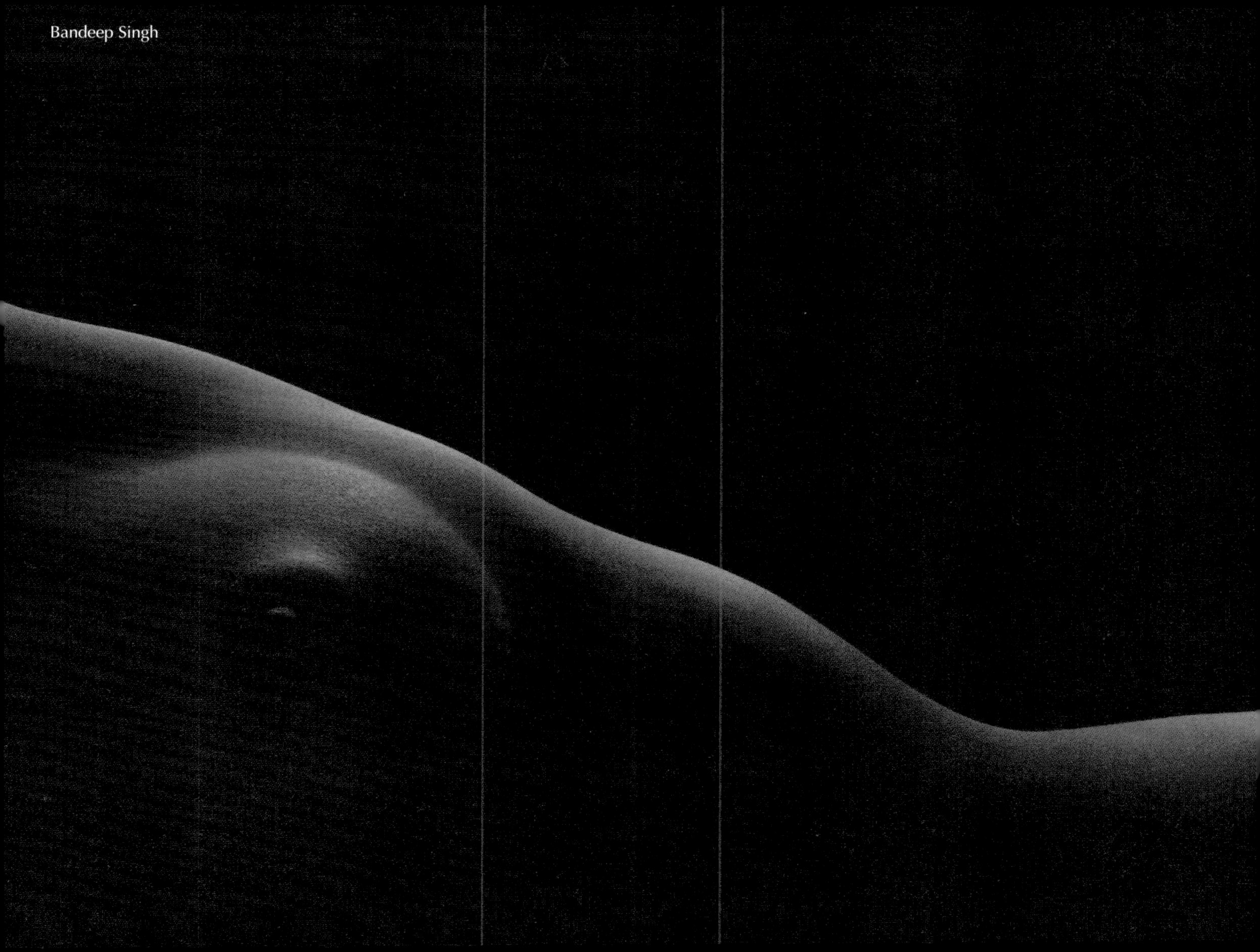

Bandeep Singh

Akash Das

Oh my generous and exuberant love
As the slow moon coldly slopes down the sky
The pines hum to themselves and you to yourself
And you pass your hands across my face.
My hands stray – stray? – to your breasts,
Small, such as angels probably are permitted.
You are forgiven, solely because of them
For beating me at Scrabble.

Dear friend you cannot know
How much you fill my days – and the long nights,
When outside the whole world is threatening silence,
The pine is swaying in a senseless dream,
Your hand within my hand, your warm warm body
Close by me, and in the dark your unseen smile.

Ashish Chawla

Sonnet: Vikram Seth

It's not that I
like wearing flowers
in my hair

nor these jewels for ear
finger hand throat ankle

(I know myself
to be most beautiful
when naked)

It's just that I like
you to
linger
removing these.

It's Just That I:
Kamla Kapur

Akash Das

'All that is best for us comes of itself in our hands –
but if we strive to overtake it,
it perpetually eludes us.'

Ananda K. Coomaraswamy

There it was,
hanging right outside
your bedroom window:

distended fruit of the
bush, its purple
skin bursting with secretions.

You opened the pane,
patiently removed the screen,
and I extended my arm –
an easy stretch.

To touch it was to have it.
It was ready
for my hand, and
ripe. Upon the tree

any longer, and the
starlings – those wise
birds who know exactly
when to feast –
would have got it.

But this fig was for me. Us.
Pink pulp beneath the purple
skin, moist meat
of the earth, manna
for all mouths.

It was the last
of the season, beloved.
The sun was shifting
its path among the stars.

May we now
taste this long
separation, and our barren
tongues: be grateful
even for our hungers.

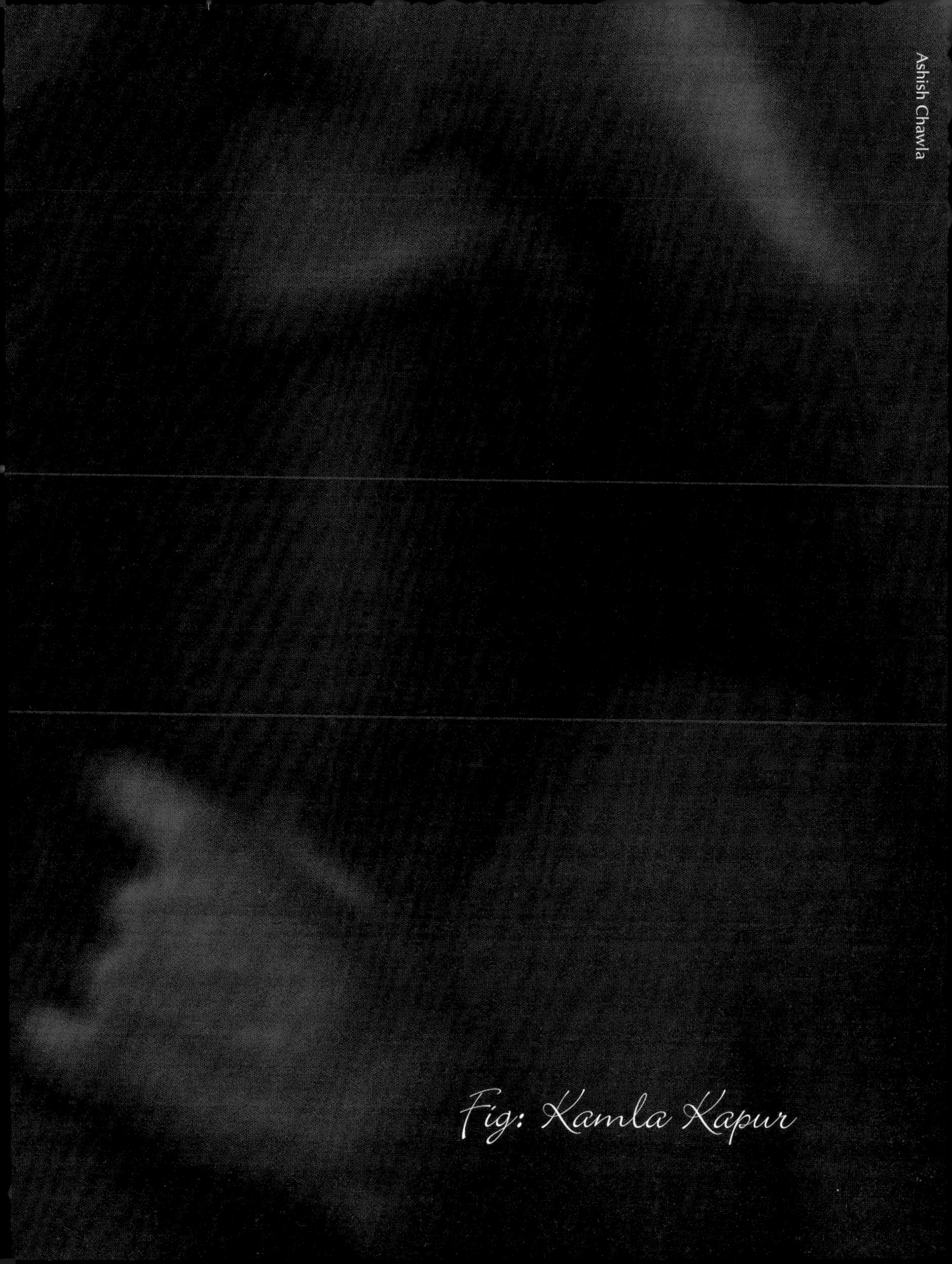

Ashish Chawla

Fig: Kamla Kapur

Lesleigh Goldberg

Unbutton your fragrant clothes of sleep and come to me
I will watch your bare white breasts burning through the
    black
tresses of desire and I will throw your silent wounds into
    the sky
Where purple birds will tear you into a woman and
    lilac shadows
will cover your wounds with the naked touch of dusk
    on their wings
there will be the feigned blue of the Godavari in your
    sleep as
you will draw your legs around mine and I will search
    for fear
and the secret syllables of grass between your breasts
    when you
will gently unbutton the fragrant clothes of sleep
    and come to me

and I shall tear the night from your womb

Unbutton Your Fragrant Clothes of Sleep and Come to Me: Pritish Nandy

Wild horses rage in your tresses on this savage night
of desire
when primal fire breaks through your loins
descend the dark mountain of sorrow tonight let a black
rain
of stars bathe your limbs in blood

wild virgin of death teach me the fury of the night
teach me to bleed and not feel pain teach me to suffer
the
anguish of words

and when the rivers of passion flow into your breasts let
me
discover the tender gold of your flesh let me wander in a
field of discreet memories

let a black rain of stars bathe your limbs in blood
tonight

Wild Horses Rage in Your Tresses: Pritish Nandy

Ashish Chawla

Akash Das

Clumps of smoke simmer in the pan, and slowly
  lift to caress the outline of your breasts

as you cook, stirring spices in carrot, milk,
  and cream – ingredients that conjure

recipes of hunger and passion. As you stroke
  sugar and butter and gently melt

flakes of grated almond-shavings,
  more clumps of perfumed smoke permeate through

the silk of your shirt – now transparent in heat –
  painting the outer circle of the nipples

to an hardened edge, tasting the sweet
  skin, the surface of the crinkled base,

to a creamed mouthful of untampered delicacy.

Indian Dessert: Sudeep Sen

Under the soft translucent linen,
  the ridges around your nipples

harden at the thought of my tongue.
  You – lying inverted like the letter 'c' –

arch yourself deliberately
  wanting the warm press of my lips,

it's wet to coat the skin
  that is bristling, burning,

breaking into sweats of desire –
  sweet juices of imagination.

But in fact, I haven't even touched
  you. At least, not yet.

Desire: Sudeep Sen

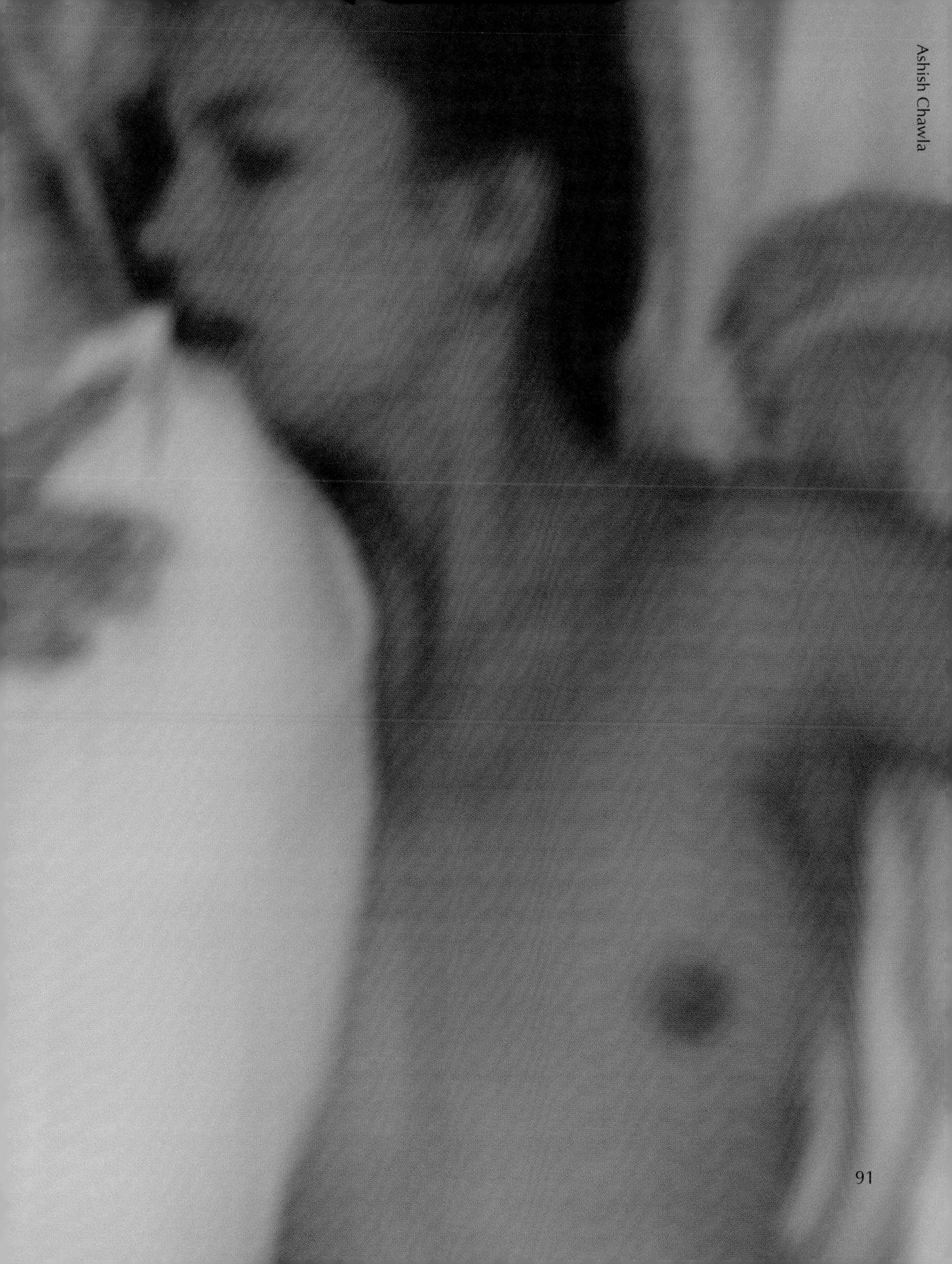

Ashish Chawla

Everything, everyone goes into that mouth.
You in that mouth, washed blue TV light,
tunnel light, cold hotel air,
food half eaten on a tray, someone there
on the carpet, sleeping maybe or tripping,
someone's cigarette saying, the way you open
your mouth like it's what, like satire but.
The slide, the pull, the come, the remark unfinished.
The pull come slides the unfinished remark
like it's open, like satire in your mouth.
The way your cigarette says someone, someone's
sleeping carpet maybe, half eaten on a tray.
Washed blue tunnel light, cold TV hotel,
you in that mouth eating everything.

Bandeep Singh

When it rains, the dead descend, you appear,
the smell of rainwater in your hair,

wearing the ring I placed on your finger,
a scent like heat and a voice not yours, a
child's voice singing of age-old danger,
in Hindi, a lover's lament from *Pyaasa*.

Your lips, clear of the color you wear,
are not new to me, are lovely and bare,

and our old argument still burns.
How soon will you forget me if I die?
By the river in this room and the way it returns,
I swear, If I forget you, let everything die.

When it rains the dead ascend, disappear
where we cannot follow, into the living air.

with a first line by Michelle Yasmin Valladares

From Premonition: Jeet Thayil

Ashish Chawla

About the photographers/artists

ASHISH CHAWLA has attempted to take photography beyond technique, and image beyond any fixed meaning, to follow his memories and fantasies that have given his body of work an extremely personal touch. His photographs make us, the viewers, traverse through a spectacular range of evocations, unravelling the fragility of human emotions. The sharpness of every hazy detail is by no means simplistic as Ashish uses his skills and experience to bring a certain special mood to every single image. His use of photography is aligned in some ways with Pictorialism, arriving at effects that are impressionistic and dreamy in nature but strangely alive, almost fierce in their power.

AKASH DAS is a big name of Indian advertising photography, and winner of more than 100 national and international awards, Akash Das has many firsts to his credit in the field of visual communication. His work has been featured in leading French and Indian magazines, and exhibited all over the world. A keen awareness of social and environmental issues has always coloured his vision. He was the first to hold a solo exhibition on the Asian elephant, and has done pioneering campaigns on social issues such as AIDS and homosexuality.

BANDEEP SINGH is a reputed photographer working as the picture editor of a leading national magazine. Known for his extremely nuanced and contemplative work, he has been deeply inspired by Zen and Sufi thought. Bandeep's new work is an exploration of the theme of eroticism from the perspective of the Indian aesthetic tradition – where the sensual and the sacred exist on the same plane. His latest body of work, 'Antarghat' – exhibited in 2008 – and celebrating the feminine form in its deep symbolic association with the elements of earth and fertility, was hugely acclaimed as 'bold', 'empowering' and 'heralding the arrival of the essential Indian photographic nude'.

KISHORE CHATTERJEE could well be called the last of the Tagore family artists. His artistic heritage can be traced to his grandmother Sunayani Devi, Tagore's niece and sister of Abanindranath Tagore, as well as the sculptress Meera Mukherjee who was his aunt and deeply influenced his work. Over the years he has painted a vast range of subjects from Indian myths to Shakespeare, clowns, dogs and owls. Kishore's work has an inherent music because he is a connoisseur of Western Classical music and an author and columnist on the subject. His work on male nudes goes back to the 1970s, and he is the only Indian artist who has held a complete solo exhibition on Beethoven (2000) and Jesus Christ (1997).

LESLEIGH GOLDBERG was born in Denver Colorado. She did her Bachelors and Masters of Fine Arts from the University of Pennsylvania. Her works have been exhibited all over the world, with major exhibitions being held at San Francisco County Museum of Art, Los Angeles County Museum of Art, Crafts Museum of New York, Museum of Contemporary Art, Cincinnati, Ohio, Gallery Carole Brimmaud, Paris, Tour De Cardineau, Isle Sur la Sorge, France, and Kimball Art Center, Park City, Utah.

SANJIB SEN is originally a trained art director, who has worked in advertising agencies for more than a decade. While his commercial photography covers subjects as varied as fashion, food, interiors, consumer products and industry, he satisfies his creative muse by shooting eclectic themes ranging from people, nature and landscapes. Sen's latest creative outpourings saw the light of day in his exhibition on the female nude held at the India Habitat Centre, New Delhi, in 2008. The selection of works in this book is from this collection.

VIKRAM BAWA has a background in math and law and spent the first eight years of his professional life running a chemicals company. But fate pointed towards another direction, and he entered the world of photography where he soon reached the top. He was the first in India to introduce 3D photography, and then subsequently, what he called 'disappearing photography'. He secured the second prize at the PMA international awards for his 3D images that became part of a 30-country exhibition. Vikram was also the first to win the best photography campaign for a five star hotel (Leela Palace Goa) in the world. His latest accolade is 'best calendar of the year 2009'. His work has been featured in over 250 magazine covers.

WASWO X. WASWO currently makes his home in Udaipur, Rajasthan, but was born in the USA, and was educated at The Milwaukee Center for Photography and Studio Marangoni, the Center for Contemporary Photography in Florence, Italy. His photographs have been featured in such publications as *Jetwings, Asian Photography, The Times Journal of Photography, Better Photography, Namaskaar, Verve* and *Serendib*. He has authored a widely distributed collection of his work that is titled *India Poems: The Photographs*. The artist's latest projects have involved hand-coloured digital prints, made at his Udaipur studio. Waswo has exhibited extensively in India and Sri Lanka, and has had solo exhibitions in Europe and the USA, including the Haggerty Museum of Art.

Lesleigh Goldberg

Copyright acknowledgements

P. 17, From *Gathasaptasati* – translated by David Ray, Copper Canyon Press, 1990.
P. 19, From *Ritusamhara*: Kalidasa – *The Loom of Time: A Selection of Plays and Poems by Kalidasa*, translated by Chandra Rajan, Penguin India.
P. 22, From *Meghaduta*: Kalidasa – *The Loom of Time: A Selection of Plays and Poems by Kalidasa*, translated by Chandra Rajan, Penguin India.
P. 25, 'Confrontations': Amarusataka – *Kamashastra in Classical Sanskrit Literature*, V. K. Hampiholi, Ajanta Publications.
P. 26, 'Unions': Amarusataka – *Kamashastra in Classical Sanskrit Literature*, V. K. Hampiholi, Ajanta Publications.
P. 32, From *Fantasies of a Love Thief*: Bilhana – translated by Barbara S. Miller.
P. 34, From *Gita Govinda*: Jayadeva – rendered from the Sanskrit by George Keyt.
P. 36, From *Gita Govinda*: Jayadeva – rendered from the Sanskrit by George Keyt.
P. 41, 'Her hair, flying loose': Vidyapati – *Oriental Erotic Art*, Philip Rawson, Quartet Books.
P. 42, From *Surativichitra Madhya*: Keshavdasa – *Rasikpriya of Keshavdasa*, translated by K. P. Bahadur, Motilaldas Banarasidas.
P. 44, 'That pert one drinks': Amir Khusro – *Khusrau ka Zahni Safar*, translated by Z. Ansari, Anjuman Taraqqi Urdu Hind.
P. 49, Couplets: Amir Khusro – *Khusrau ka Zahni Safar*, translated by Z. Ansari, Anjuman Taraqqi Urdu Hind.
P. 50, *Haqiqat al Fuqara* (Folio 50) – *Same-Sex Love in India – Readings in Indian Literature*, Ed. Ruth Vanita and Saleem Kidwai.
P. 53, *Haqiqat al Fuqara* (Folio 52) – *Same-Sex Love in India – Readings in Indian Literature*, Ed. Ruth Vanita and Saleem Kidwai.
P. 58, 'Champak Blossoms': Sarojini Naidu – *The Sceptred Flute – Songs of India*, Kitabistan.
P. 61, 'The Virgin': Amrita Pritam – Translated from Punjabi by Kartar Singh Duggal.
P. 63, 'The Looking Glass': Kamala Das – *The Old Playhouse and Other Poems*, Orient Longman.
P. 65, 'The Stone Age': Kamala Das – *The Old Playhouse and Other Poems*, Orient Longman.
P. 69, 'Distance': Gulzar – *Selected Poems of Gulzar*, translated by Pavan K. Varma, Penguin India.
P. 70, 'At Khajuraho' – Reprinted by permission of David Ray.
P. 72, Ghazal: Javed Akhtar – *Quiver – Poems and Ghazals*, translated by David Matthews, Harper Collins India.
P. 76, Sonnet: Vikram Seth – *Collected Poems*, Penguin India.
P. 78, 'It's Just That I' – Reprinted by permission of Kamla Kapur.
P. 80, 'Fig' – Reprinted by permission of Kamla Kapur.
P. 83, 84, Reprinted by permission of Pritish Nandy.
P. 88, 'Indian Dessert': Sudeep Sen; P. 90, 'Desire': Sudeep Sen
Copyright ©SUDEEP SEN. Reprinted with the permission of the author. These poems are part of a longer sequence of poems that appeared as books: Lines of Desire [USA: University of South Carolina], and Prayer Flag [USA: Wings Press / UK: Peepal Tree]. They also appear in Indian Love Poems [USA: Knopf / UK: Everyman Library], and werebroadcast on BBC, CNN, IBN, NDTV & AIR. Some of the pieces have been set to music and performed by 'Advaita' [New Delhi] and by 'Javier Coble Quartet' [Madrid].
P. 93, 'Sonnets for the Mouth': Jeet Thayil – Reprinted by permission of Jeet Thayil.
P. 95, 'Premonition 10' – *These Errors Are Correct*, Tranquebar, New Delhi. Reprinted by permission of Jeet Thayil.